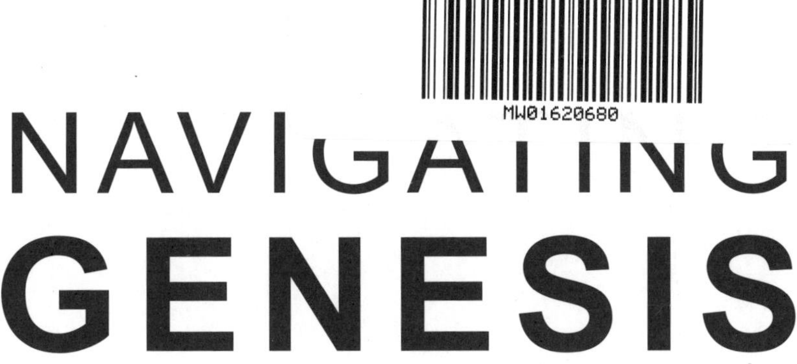


# NAVIGATING GENESIS

## Study Guide

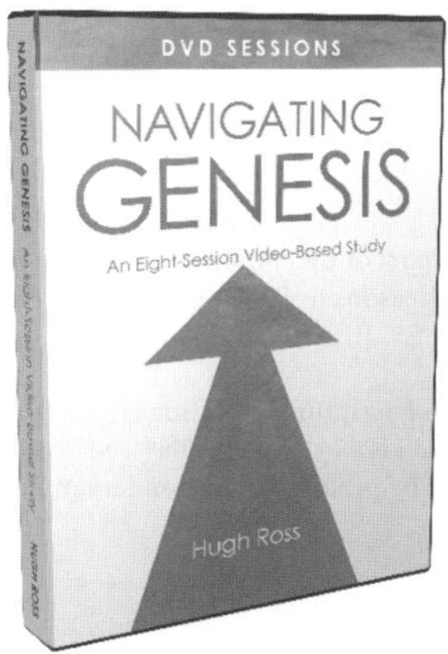


An Eight-Session Video-Based Study
for Groups or Individuals

(855) REASONS | www.reasons.org

# Contents

Welcome 5

Session 1 – Is Putting Science and the Bible Together a Bad Idea? 9

Session 2 – Does the Big Bang Contradict the Bible? 19

Session 3 – Did Life Evolve from a Primordial Soup? 27

Session 4 – Doesn't the Bible Contradict Science? 35

Session 5 – Does the Fossil Record Prove Evolution? 45

Session 6 – Did Humans Evolve from Apes? 53

Session 7 – Why Does God Rest? 61

Session 8 – Does Genesis 2 Conflict with Genesis 1? 69

Outreach Challenges 77

Where Do We Go from Here? 93

# Welcome

We invite you to embark on an amazing journey to catch a captivating glimpse of the Creator's glory, power, wisdom, and love. The *Navigating Genesis* study offers a unique opportunity to explore powerful evidences for the reliability and trustworthiness of Scripture—and its supernatural Author.

The twenty-first century has brought many new challenges to belief in the accuracy and authority of the Bible, and of Genesis in particular. Yet, instead of offering an excuse for disbelief and rejection, the early chapters of Genesis present some of the most persuasive evidences ever assembled for the supernatural authorship, accuracy, and authority of Scripture.

Inspired by Hugh Ross's book *Navigating Genesis*, this study has been designed as a tool to help build Christians' confidence in the evidence on which their faith stands and to equip them to share their faith with nonbelieving family and friends.

It is our hope that this study will also serve as a way for you, your group, and your church to get to know the ministry of Reasons to Believe. Our organization exists to engage secular influencers (such as scientists and professors) with current scientific support for Scripture, to equip believers to defend their faith with gentleness and respect, and to empower the church to spread the gospel by providing apologetics tools believers can use with confidence and effectiveness.

As you progress through the study, we hope your group will experience a deeper level of trust in the reliability of the Bible. May you be inspired to join us in reaching out to those who are curious, questioning, and hungry for the truth.

— The Reasons to Believe Team

# SESSION 1

## Is Putting Science and the Bible Together a Bad Idea?

# SESSION 1
# Is Putting Science and the Bible Together a Bad Idea?

## Focus Verse

*But in your hearts set apart Christ as Lord. Always be prepared to give an answer to everyone who asks you to give the reason for the hope that you have. But do this with gentleness and respect.*

1 Peter 3:15

## Starting the Conversation

We're beginning our study by talking about whether it's even a good idea to put science and faith together. Many people, including some Christians, think that science and faith are like oil and water—they simply *can't* (or at least shouldn't)—be mixed together.

Astronomer and pastor Dr. Hugh Ross, the teacher in this series, has spent over three decades demonstrating to believers and nonbelievers alike that there is a reasonable and responsible way to integrate the record of nature with the words of the Bible—without compromising the integrity of either.

In this week's video presentation, Dr. Ross will outline his strategy for integration.

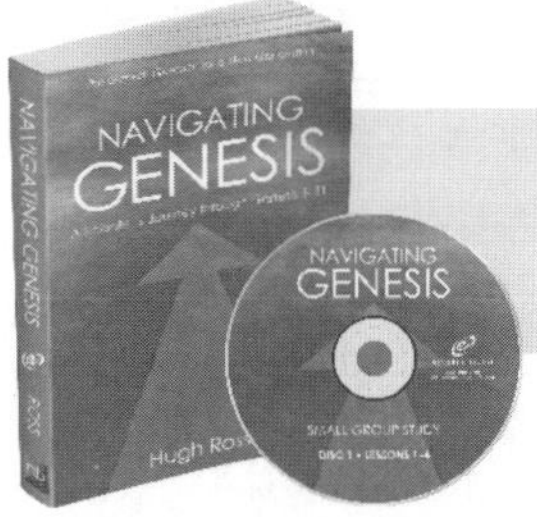


**Watch video lesson 1 now and follow along in your outline.**

## Session Outline

### › Categories of scientific evidences influential to Dr. Ross as a young man

- Origin of the universe
- Design of the universe (anthropic principle)
- Fossil record
- Origin of humans

The Bible's harmony with science led to Dr. Ross's conversion to Christianity.

### › Fears people have about putting the Bible and science together

**FEAR #1**

Genesis 1–11 damages the gospel's credibility.

*Answer:* Genesis 1 and science *can* fit together!

**God Cannot Lie or Deceive**

| | |
|---|---|
| Numbers 23:19 | Romans 3:4 |
| Psalm 12:6 | Hebrews 6:18 |
| Psalm 19:7–8 | Titus 1:2 |
| Psalm 119:160 | 1 John 1:5 |
| Proverbs 30:5 | |

***Notes***

Nature – Created by God
Bible – Inspired by God
Science – Human interpretation of the facts of nature
Theology – Human interpretation of the Bible's words

Our knowledge of both theology and science is incomplete. We all have biases and make mistakes. Therefore *apparent* conflicts between science and theology happen. How do we determine which interpretations are correct?

> *But examine everything carefully; hold fast to that which is good.*
> 1 Thessalonians 5:21 (NASB)

**FEAR #2**

The theme of redemption will be eclipsed if too much attention is given to science.

*Answer:* The best way to understand both the Bible and science is to connect creation and redemption.

> *[He] who has saved us and called us to a holy life—not because of anything we have done but because of his own purpose and grace. This grace was given us in Christ Jesus before the beginning of time.*
> 2 Timothy 1:9

**Notes**

*A faith and knowledge resting on the hope of eternal life, which God, who does not lie, promised before the beginning of time.*
Titus 1:2

**FEAR #3**

Creation controversies result in division within the church.

*Answer:* The best way to resolve a church controversy is to discuss differences respectfully.

Peacemaking vs. peacekeeping

### › Why putting science with the Bible is a great idea

1. Integrating Genesis with science will enhance the gospel's credibility.
2. Scripture consistently links creation and redemption.
3. Creation reveals the attributes of God as well as His plans and purposes.

*For since the creation of the world God's invisible qualities—his eternal power and divine nature—have been clearly seen, being understood from what has been made, so that men are without excuse.*
Romans 1:20

***Notes***

> *And without faith it is impossible to please God, because anyone who comes to him must believe that he exists and that he rewards those who earnestly seek him.*
>
> Hebrews 11:6

**Notes**

If you want to lead someone into a relationship with the Creator of the universe…

- Step #1: Establish the existence of God.
- Step #2: Establish that God desires good for those who come to Him.

Science is a crucial tool for evangelism.

## The Bottom Line

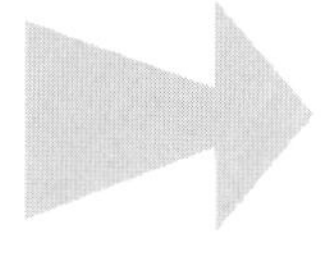

Evangelical Christians often struggle to share their faith with nonbelievers, but science offers an effective tool to help bring people to faith in Jesus as their Creator and Savior.

## Reflection

Discuss the following questions together. Consider sharing relevant personal experiences so others can benefit from your situation.

- Read through the Focus Verse together. Do you feel prepared to answer tough faith questions? If so, what steps have you taken to get prepared?
- Can you think of a time when you avoided a conversation in which someone asked difficult questions about your faith in Jesus? If so, share one specific question from that conversation that stumped you.
- What are some ways you can make peace (encourage respectful dialogue) in-

stead of merely keeping peace (avoiding tough topics) when difficult discussions about faith arise?

Want to explore more science? Visit **reasons.org/navigatinggenesis** for additional articles, videos, and podcasts on themes related to this lesson.

## Outreach Challenge

As part of your journey through the *Navigating Genesis* study, we want to empower you to share your faith with nonbelievers. The back of this guide contains a series of Outreach Challenges to help facilitate this goal. We think these optional exercises will enhance your ability to build connections with non-Christians.

- Read through Outreach Challenge #1 (p. 79) as a group.
- Share your thoughts about the challenge. What concerns do you have? What would prevent you from participating?

## Going Deeper

- These video sessions are based on Dr. Ross's book *Navigating Genesis*. If you'd like to explore the themes from this lesson in more detail, we suggest reading chapters 1–2.
- Download this week's FREE resource from RTB. In this audio message, Dr. Ross shares the story of how his scientist's curiosity led him to investigate the Bible and come to faith in Jesus Christ. To download this resource, visit **shop.reasons.org**, click on "Audio," and then scroll down to find *An Astronomer's Quest* (MP3). Add it to your cart and use the coupon code **NavGenS1** at checkout.
- Throughout the week, reread this session's Focus Verse as part of your daily devotions. Challenge yourself to memorize it before your next group meeting.

Consider sharing one thing you learned this week or a favorite quote from the ***Navigating Genesis*** book on Facebook or Twitter.

**Use #navgen**

# SESSION 2

## Does the Big Bang Contradict the Bible?

# SESSION 2
# Does the Big Bang Contradict the Bible?

## Focus Verse

*In the beginning God created the heavens and the earth.*

Genesis 1:1

## Starting the Conversation

Last week, Dr. Ross started us on our search for harmony between Scripture and nature by explaining his method of integration. This week he will apply that framework to the question: **Where did the universe come from?**

You probably learned in school that the universe started with the big bang.

- Have you ever wondered how the big bang fits with the Bible? Or if it contradicts the Bible?
- What have you heard others say about the big bang?
- Is your impression of the big bang mostly positive, negative, or neutral?

In this week's video session, Dr. Ross will compare data about the origin of the universe from both the biblical and scientific realms.

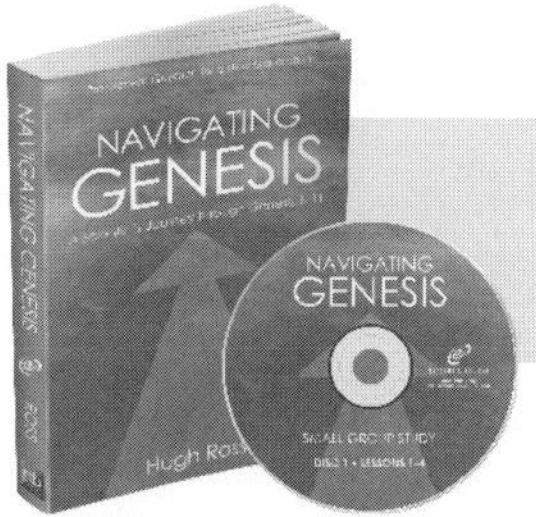


**Watch video lesson 2 now and follow along in your outline.**

## Session Outline

### › Does the big bang contradict the Bible?

**Fears about the big bang**

- Fear #1: The big bang is the foundation for biological evolution.
- Fear #2: The big bang might undermine the Bible's credibility.

**History check**

When the big bang theory was first proposed, many scientists rejected it because it too closely resembled the *biblical* account of creation and it didn't allow enough time for evolution. Many embraced the big bang only after evidence for it became too overwhelming to ignore.

### › Cosmic claims of the Bible

**1. Space and time had a beginning**

- *Scripture says:*

| | |
|---|---|
| Genesis 1:1 | Isaiah 45:18 |
| Genesis 2:3–4 | John 1:3 |
| Psalm 148:5 | Colossians 1:15–17 |
| Isaiah 40:26 | Hebrews 11:3 |
| Isaiah 42:5 | |

- *Science says:* A Causal Agent transcends space and time.

**Notes**

**2. The universe is expanding from a beginning.**

- *Scripture says:*

  Job 9:8
  Psalm 104:2
  Isaiah 40:22
  Isaiah 42:5
  Isaiah 44:24
  Isaiah 45:12
  Isaiah 48:13
  Isaiah 51:13
  Jeremiah 10:12
  Jeremiah 51:15
  Zechariah 12:1

- *Science says:* The universe is expanding from a beginning.

**3. The physical laws are constant.**

- *Scripture says:* God established the fixed laws of heaven and earth (Jeremiah 33:25).

- *Science says:* The universe is governed by fine-tuned physical laws.

**4. The universe is undergoing pervasive decay.**

- *Scripture says:* The creation itself will be liberated from its bondage to decay (Romans 8:20–22).

- *Science says:* Life would be impossible without a level of pervasive decay.

***Notes***

## *The Bottom Line*

Some Christians fear that the big bang might undermine the credibility of the Bible, but upon closer examination what the big bang says about the beginning of the universe is consistent with what the Bible tells us about creation.

## Reflection

Discuss the following questions together as a group. Consider sharing relevant personal experiences so others can benefit from your situation.

- Did anyone in your group memorize the Focus Verse from session 1 (1 Peter 3:15)? Take a moment to say the verse aloud together. If you don't have it memorized quite yet, try again next week.
- Prior to this session, what were your thoughts on the big bang? What about now? Has learning about the big bang strengthened your confidence in the belief that God created the universe? If so, how?
- Describe a science-Scripture connection you made as a result of this session that you hadn't seen before.
- Share a question with the group that you still have about the big bang and its possible connection to the Bible. The Going Deeper section will direct you to some additional resources.

Want to explore more science? Visit **reasons.org/navigatinggenesis** for additional articles, videos, and podcasts on themes related to this lesson.

## Prayer

- If you did Outreach Challenge #1, look over the list of people you committed to pray for during this study. Continue to pray for those people each day. Ask God to prepare them to hear the good news of Jesus as their Savior and Creator.
- Ask God to give you the courage to share the gospel with others and to provide you with opportunities to do it.
- Pray together for your group's specific requests.

## Outreach Challenge

We want to continue encouraging you to share your faith. Again, these challenges are optional, but they can help you grow in your ability to build connections with nonbelievers.

Take a minute right now to read through Outreach Challenge #2 (p. 81) as a group.

We encourage you to arrange a meet-up with one of the people on your prayer list. What feelings do you experience as you imagine doing this challenge? Share your thoughts with the group.

## Going Deeper

- The video sessions are based on Dr. Ross's book *Navigating Genesis*. If you'd like to explore the themes from this lesson in more detail, we suggest reading chapter 3.
- Download this week's FREE resource from RTB. In this audio message, you'll hear JPL physicist Dr. Dave Rogstad discuss more about the evidence for the big bang creation event. To download this resource, visit **shop.reasons.org**, click on "Audio," and then scroll down to find *Big Bang or Big Fraud?* (MP3). Add it to your cart and use the coupon code **NavGenS2** at checkout.

---

Consider sharing one thing you learned this week or a favorite quote from the ***Navigating Genesis*** book on Facebook or Twitter.

**Use #navgen**

---

# SESSION 3

## Did Life Evolve from a Primordial Soup?

# SESSION 3
# Did Life Evolve from a Primordial Soup?

## Focus Verse

*Now the earth was formless and empty, darkness was over the surface of the deep, and the Spirit of God was hovering over the waters.*

Genesis 1:2

## Starting the Conversation

We're continuing our search for the harmony between Scripture and nature. In this session we will explore the **origin of life on early Earth.**

You probably learned in school that the first life (bacteria) originated a few billion years ago in an ancient primordial soup. Science textbooks generally describe the early Earth as being covered in water brimming with prebiotic elements just waiting for the right conditions to come together and form the first life.

- Did you ever study the Miller-Urey experiment in biology class (early Earth + water + lightning + chemistry = life)? What did you learn?
- Have you ever wondered, how does the primordial soup scenario that I learned in school fit or conflict with the Bible?
- What do you think: does evolution make God unnecessary if all it takes is the right chemistry for life to begin?

In this week's video presentation, Dr. Ross will compare data about the origin of Earth's first life from both the biblical and scientific realms.

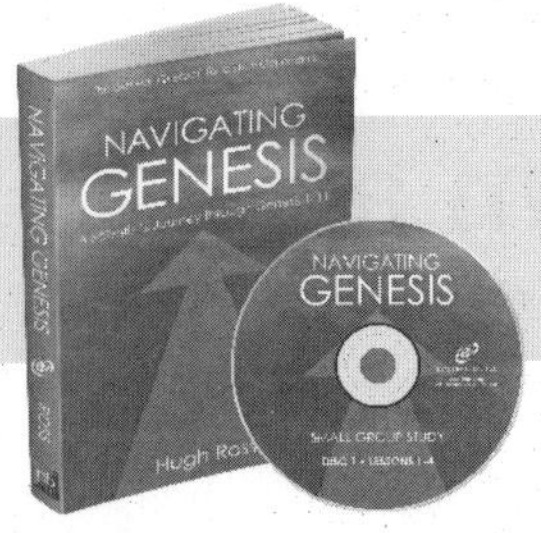

**Watch video lesson 3 now and follow along in your outline.**

## Session Outline

### › Did life evolve from a primordial soup?

**Naturalism's story for the first life**

Predictions

- Darwin: "small warm pond"
- The early Earth contained a huge concentrated soup of life's building blocks.
- Life evolved after an enormous amount of time.
- Life evolved under benign conditions.
- Result: LUCA (last universal common ancestor)

**Biblical story for the first life**

> *Now the earth was formless*
> *and empty, darkness was over*
> *the surface of the deep, and*
> *the Spirit of God was hovering*
> [rāḥap] *over the waters.*
>
> Genesis 1:2

***Notes***

**Initial conditions**

- It was dark.
- The Earth was covered with water.

**Predictions**

- Life originated early.
- Life originated under hostile conditions.
- First life was complex, diverse, and abundant.
- First life was marine life.
- First life was the result of miraculous intervention.

---

**› Which story fits best with the scientific evidence?**

---

**What science reveals**

- Life appeared early.
- Life appeared abundantly, as soon as Earth's conditions allowed for life to survive.
- No evidence exists for an ancient prebiotic soup.
- There is no resolution to the oxygen/UV crisis.
- The first life was chemically complex.

**The story of Nobel Laureate Rick Smalley**

**How long are the creation days in Genesis 1?**

- Part of the daylight hours
- All of the daylight hours
- 24-hour period
- Long, but finite period of time

***Notes***

## The Bottom Line

The latest scientific evidence challenges the evolutionary scenario for the origin of life and is consistent with the biblical account of God creating all life.

## Reflection

Discuss the following questions together as a group. Consider sharing relevant personal experiences so others can benefit from your situation.

- Did anyone in your group memorize the Focus Verse from session 1 (1 Peter 3:15)? Take a moment to say the verse aloud together.
- What were your thoughts on the origin of life before watching the video presentation? What about now?
- What difference does it make if the first life was created rather than evolved from natural processes? How might this be useful in conversations with non-Christians?
- Describe a science-Scripture connection you made as a result of this session.

Want to explore more science? Visit **reasons.org/navigatinggenesis** for additional articles, videos, and podcasts on themes related to this lesson.

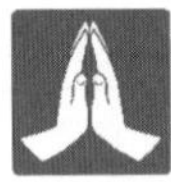

## Prayer

- Ask God to give you the courage to share the gospel with others and to provide you with opportunities to do it.
- Pray together for your group's specific requests.

## Outreach Challenge

- If you completed Outreach Challenge #2, report your experience to the group. How did it go? What did you expect to happen? What *actually* happened?
- If you didn't have time last week to complete the challenge, that's okay. Consider trying again this week. If you're nervous about attempting this challenge, share what's holding you back with the group.

## Going Deeper

- The video sessions are based on Dr. Ross's book *Navigating Genesis*. If you'd like to explore the themes from this lesson in more detail, we suggest reading Appendix A.
- Download this week's FREE resource from RTB. In this audio message, biochemist Dr. Fazale (Fuz) Rana shares how studying cells in graduate school started him on the journey that led him to faith in Jesus. To download, visit **shop.reasons.org**, click on "Audio," and then scroll down to find *Finding God in the Lab* (MP3). Add it to your cart and use the coupon code **NavGenS3** at checkout.

---

Consider sharing one thing you learned this week or a favorite quote from the ***Navigating Genesis*** book on Facebook or Twitter.

**Use #navgen**

---

# SESSION 4

## Doesn't the Bible Contradict Science?

# SESSION 4
# Doesn't the Bible Contradict Science?

## Focus Verse

*How many are your works, O Lord! In wisdom you made them all; the earth is full of your creatures.*

Psalm 104:24

## Starting the Conversation

We're continuing our search for the harmony between Scripture and nature. We've already learned about some major events in the history of creation—and yet we've covered only the first two verses of the Bible. We haven't even started discussing the "days" of creation yet!

In this session, we'll explore the **first four days of creation** and several common objections that atheists raise about the Bible's **scientific accuracy**. If you ever talk to a scientist or skeptic about creation, they're likely to point out that the order of events described in Genesis 1 is in conflict with the scientific record.

- Take a few minutes to read Genesis 1:3–19 aloud. Together, make a list of events that you think happened on each day of creation.
- What did you discover from doing this exercise?

In this week's video presentation, Dr. Ross will offer a proposal for reconciling the days of creation with the scientific record.

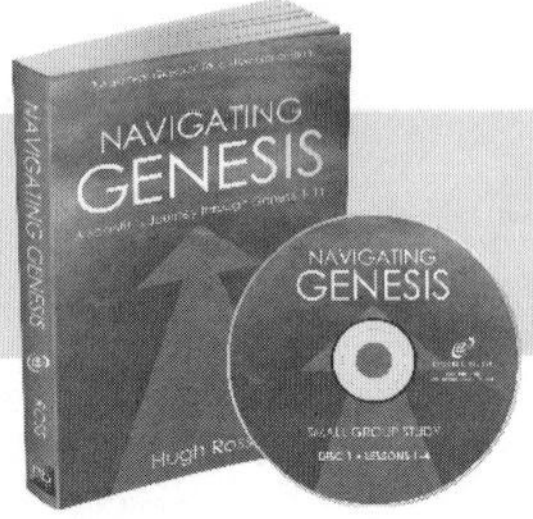


**Watch video lesson 4 now and follow along in your outline.**

## Session Outline

> **Doesn't the Bible contradict science?**
> **Are the events of creation days 1–4 in the wrong order?**

**Keys to Bible interpretation**

1. Have the correct frame of reference
   - Genesis 1 tells the creation events from the point of view of Earth's surface (not outer space).
2. Determine the initial conditions
   - The early Earth was dark.
   - The early Earth was covered with water.
   - The early Earth was empty of life.
   - The early Earth was unfit for life.

**What happened on each creation day?**

***Notes***

**Creation Day 1**

*And God said, "Let there be light," and there was light...God called the light "day," and the darkness he called "night."*

Genesis 1:3, 5a

*When I made the clouds its garment and wrapped it in thick darkness.*

Job 38:9

Creation miracle: Transformation of the atmosphere from opaque to translucent (semi-transparent); sunlight is visible, but the sky remains overcast

**Creation Day 2**

*And God said, "Let there be a vault between the waters to separate water from water."... God called the vault "sky."*

Genesis 1:6, 8a

Creation miracle: Formation of the water cycle

**Creation Day 3**

*And God said, "Let the water under the sky be gathered to one place, and let dry ground appear." And it was so. God*

**Notes**

> *called the dry ground "land," and the gathered waters he called "seas."*
>
> Genesis 1:9–10a

Creation miracle: Formation of landmasses

Skeptic's Challenge: Did animals precede plants?

> *Then God said, "Let the land produce vegetation* [deshe']*: seed-bearing plants and trees on the land that bear fruit with seed in it, according to their various kinds." And it was so.*
>
> Genesis 1:11

Creation miracle: Appearance of land plants

Visit **reasons.org/navigatinggenesis** for more of Dr. Ross's thoughts regarding early plants.

**Creation Day 4**

Skeptic's Challenge: Were the Sun, Moon, and stars created on day 4?

> *And God said, "Let there be lights in the expanse of the heavens to separate the day from the night. And let them be for signs and for seasons, and for days and years, and let them be lights*

**Notes**

*in the expanse of the heavens to give light upon the earth." And it was so. And God made the two great lights—the greater light to rule the day and the lesser light to rule the night—and the stars.*
Genesis 1:14–16 (ESV)

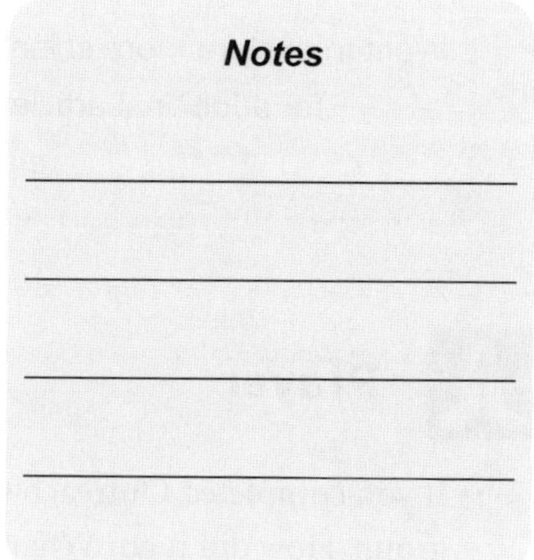

Creation miracle: Transformation of the atmosphere from translucent to transparent; Sun, Moon, and stars became visible.

**Notes**

## The Bottom Line

Skeptics often raise the concern that the events of Genesis 1 are in the wrong order, but if this passage's primary point of view is the planet's surface, then the chronology of Genesis 1 matches what science tells us about Earth's history.

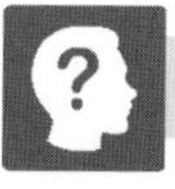

## Reflection

Discuss the following questions together as a group. Consider sharing relevant personal experiences so others can benefit from your situation.

- Did anyone in your group memorize the Focus Verse from session 1 (1 Peter 3:15)? Take a moment to say the verse aloud.
- Have you ever discussed Genesis 1 with a skeptic? If so, share your experience with the group. What questions came up? Did you feel equipped to engage in that conversation?
- Did this session increase your trust in the reliability of Genesis 1? How might the information discussed in the video presentation change the way you talk with non-Christians about alleged contradictions in the Bible?
- Describe a science-Scripture connection you made as a result of this session.

Want to explore more science? Visit **reasons.org/navigatinggenesis** for additional articles, videos, and podcasts on themes related to this lesson.

## Prayer

- If you completed Outreach Challenge #2, report your experience to the group. How did it go? What did you expect to happen? What *actually* happened?
- Ask God to provide you with opportunities to share your faith with someone this week.
- Pray together for your group's specific requests.

## Outreach Challenge

Back in session 1, we said that evangelism had two key components: *preparation* and *prayer*. Outreach Challenge #3 is about working on the preparation. Take a minute right now to read through Outreach Challenge #3 (p. 85) as a group. Then think of a question that you'd like to investigate. Share your thoughts about the challenge with the group. What would prevent you from participating?

## Going Deeper

- Read through Job 38–39 and note the various descriptions of the water cycle that appear. How many can you find?
- The video sessions are based on Dr. Ross's book *Navigating Genesis*. If you'd like to explore the themes from this lesson in more detail, we suggest reading chapters 4–5 and 21.
- Download this week's FREE resource from RTB. In this audio message, you'll hear Dr. Ross discuss the foundation for the fossil deposits that pre-

pared the way for humans. To download this resource, visit **shop.reasons.org**, click on "Audio," and then scroll down to find *Why the Fossil Record Is the Way It Is* (MP3). Add it to your cart and use the coupon code **NavGenS4** at checkout.

---

Consider sharing one thing you learned this week or a favorite quote from the ***Navigating Genesis*** book on Facebook or Twitter.

**Use #navgen**

---

# SESSION 5

## Does the Fossil Record Prove Evolution?

SESSION 5

# Does the Fossil Record Prove Evolution?

## Focus Verse

*For this is what the Lord says—he who created the heavens, he is God; he who fashioned and made the earth, he founded it; he did not create it to be empty, but formed it to be inhabited—he says: "I am the Lord, and there is no other."*

Isaiah 45:18

## Starting the Conversation

We're continuing our search for the harmony between Scripture and nature. In this session, we'll be investigating **day 5** and the **first half of day 6**.

- Take a few minutes to read Genesis 1:20–25 aloud. As a group, make a list of all the creatures described on day 5 and the first half of day 6. This is the Bible's first mention of multicellular animal life.

In school you probably learned that the complex diversity of animal life that we see in the fossil record resulted from biological evolution (descent from a common ancestor).

- What arguments have you heard that use the fossil record as evidence for evolution?
- Have you ever wondered whether God used evolution as a mechanism for creation?

In this week's video presentation, Dr. Ross will explore how the biblical description of creation days 5 and 6 fits with the scientific record.

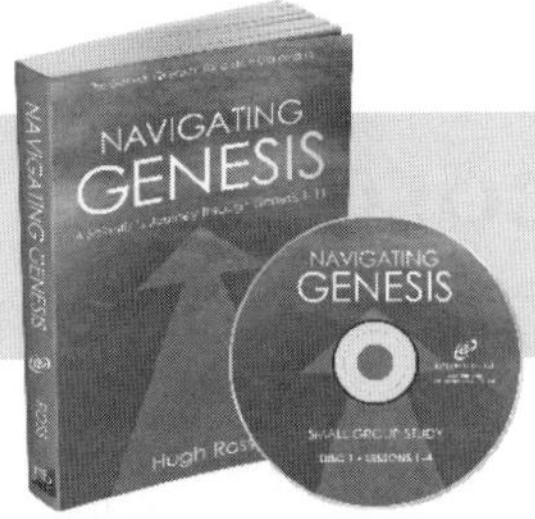

**Watch video lesson 5 now and follow along in your outline.**

## Session Outline

- **Does the fossil record prove evolution?**
- **What happened on creation day 5?**

**Notes**

**What naturalists say**

- Gradual appearance of evolutionary links between unicellular life and animals

**What scientific research is telling us about the first complex, multicellular life**

- Appears 543 million years ago
- Sudden appearance of 50–80% of all present phyla, including chordates
- Phyla appear within a brief 2–3-million-year window
- Fails to fit evolutionary trees

**Second origin of life: life that is both physical and "soulish"**

- *bārā'* = to create
- *nepesh* = soulish life
- *'āśâ* = do, fashion, accomplish, make

**Creation Day 5 miracles (Genesis 1:20–21)**

Creation of birds

*And let birds fly above the earth across the expanse of the sky." So God created...every winged bird according to its kind. And God saw that it was good.*

Genesis 1:20b, 21b

Creation of sea mammals

*And God said, "Let the water teem with living creatures"...So God created the great creatures of the sea and every living and moving thing with which the water teems, according to their kinds...And God saw that it was good.*

Genesis 1:20a, 21a

What about dinosaurs?

- Possibly created in the middle of day 5
- Lived 250 to 65 million years ago

Skeptic's Challenge: The fossil record contradicts creation days 5 and 6.

**Creation Day 6 miracle**

3 kinds of advanced land mammals created

- Small furry mammals (*remeś*)
- Livestock, herbivores (*behēmâ*)
- Wild animals; carnivores (*hayyâ*)

**Notes**

*And God said, "Let the land produce living creatures according to their kinds: the livestock* [behēmâ], *the creatures that move along the ground* [remeś], *and the wild animals* [hayyâ], *each according to its kind." And it was so. God made the wild animals according to their kinds, the livestock according to their kinds, and all the creatures that move along the ground according to their kinds. And God saw that it was good.*

Genesis 1:24–25

**Notes**

## The Bottom Line

The fossil record reveals that there were repeated, sudden appearances of complex animals, which fail to fit the theory of gradual evolution (descent from a common ancestor).

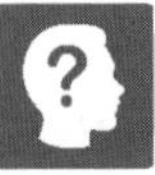

## Reflection

Discuss the following questions together as a group. Consider sharing relevant personal experiences so others can benefit from your situation.

- Did anyone in your group memorize the Focus Verse from session 1 (1 Peter 3:15)? Take a moment to say the verse aloud.
- Was this the first time you heard of the Cambrian explosion? Do you think this event provides a challenge to the evolutionary paradigm?
- What questions do you still have about evolution? The Going Deeper section will direct you to some additional resources.
- Describe a science-Scripture connection you made as a result of this session.

Want to explore more science? Visit **reasons.org/navigatinggenesis** for additional articles, videos, and podcasts on themes related to this lesson.

## Prayer

- If you completed Outreach Challenge #3 this week, report on your experience to the group. What topic did you research? What did you learn?
- Ask God to provide you with opportunities to share your faith with someone this week. Report to the group any updates about the people on your prayer list, including any conversations you've had.
- Pray together for your group's specific requests.

## Outreach Challenge

Outreach Challenge #4 highlights two key components of evangelism: *preparation* and *prayer*. We want to encourage you to engage in the ancient spiritual discipline of fasting as practiced throughout the Bible. Take a minute right now to read through Outreach Challenge #4 (p. 87). Share your thoughts with the group about the challenge. What concerns do you have about it?

## Going Deeper

- Read through Job 38–39 again. This time explore the variety of *nepesh* (soulish) creatures described there.
- The video sessions are based on Dr. Ross's book *Navigating Genesis*. If you'd like to explore the themes from this lesson in more detail, we suggest reading chapters 6 and 22.
- Download this week's FREE resource from RTB. In this booklet, Dr. Ross joins his colleague Dr. Fazale (Fuz) Rana to bring us up-to-date on key scientific discoveries that have undermined Darwinian evolution since Charles

Darwin first published his theory in the 1800s. To download this resource, visit **shop.reasons.org**, click on "Booklets," and then scroll down to find *What Darwin Didn't Know* (PDF). Add it to your cart and use the coupon code **NavGenS5** at checkout.

---

Consider sharing one thing you learned this week or a favorite quote from the ***Navigating Genesis*** book on Facebook or Twitter.

**Use #navgen**

---

# SESSION 6

## Did Humans Evolve from Apes?

# SESSION 6
# Did Humans Evolve from Apes?

## Focus Verse

*So God created mankind in his own image, in the image of God he created them; male and female he created them.*

Genesis 1:27

## Starting the Conversation

We're continuing the conversation we started in the last session about the events of creation day 6. In particular, we'll focus on the creation of **Adam and Eve**, the first humans.

- Take a minute to read Genesis 1:26–28 aloud. This is the Bible's first mention of human life.

In school you probably learned that modern humans evolved from ancient ape-like ancestors (called hominids or bipedal primates).

- Have you ever wondered whether God used evolution as a mechanism for creation? Share your current thoughts about human evolution.
- Do you remember the first time you were introduced to the idea that humans evolved from an ancient ape-like ancestor? What was your reaction?
- What do you hope to gain from this week's session on human evolution?

In this week's video presentation, Dr. Ross will discuss the harmony between nature and Scripture as it pertains to human origins.

**Watch video lesson 6 now and follow along in your outline.**

## Session Outline

### › Did humans evolve from apes?

**Genesis 1 teaches three distinct origins of life**

1. Physical life
2. Physical–soulish life
3. Physical–soulish–spiritual life (humans)

**The naturalist's story**

- Bacteria gradually evolved into humans through natural processes over long periods of time.

**The problem of probability**

- What is the probability that evolution produced intelligent life?

**How do we get consciousness from nonconsciousness?**

- The law of cause and effect teaches that the effects cannot be greater than their causes.
- The created cannot be greater than the Creator.

***Notes***

**Defining our terms**

- "cavemen"
- "Cro-Magnons"
- "*Homo sapiens*" vs. "*Homo sapiens sapiens*"
- "bipedal primate"

Notes

## › What does scientific research reveal?

**Bipedal primates**

- Small populations
- Simple tools
- Fossil record does not show gradual descent (evolutionary tree)
- Fossil record shows a sudden appearance followed by a time of stasis (no change) and then disappearance.

***Homo erectus***

- 200,000 years ago to ~2 million years ago
- DNA cannot be extracted from fossils because they are too decayed.
- Physical characteristics remain unchanged over time.

**Neanderthals**

- 48,000 years ago to 150,000 years ago
- Physical characteristics remain unchanged over time.
- Genetically distinct from humans (*Homo sapiens sapiens*)

**Adam and Eve**

- God's final creation miracle
- The only spiritual beings created on Earth
- Ancestors to all humans
- Cultural "big bangs"

**Harmony between science and the Bible**

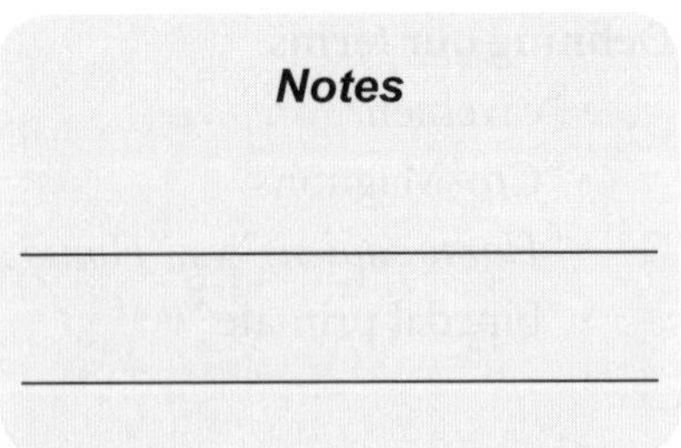


**DNA analysis**

- Consistent with humanity's origin from one man and one woman
- Arose from one region

## *The Bottom Line*

Scientific research is consistent with the major features of the biblical story of human origins.

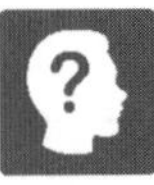

## Reflection

Discuss the following questions together as a group. Consider sharing relevant personal experiences so others can benefit from your situation.

- Did anyone in your group memorize the Focus Verse from session 1 (1 Peter 3:15)? Take a moment to say the verse aloud.
- How do you feel knowing that God prepared Earth for the benefit of all humans? How does that impact your faith?
- Share your thoughts on human origins in light of this session.
- How does this information change your perspective on modern science? Are you more open to it?

Want to explore more science? Visit **reasons.org/navigatinggenesis** for additional articles, videos, and podcasts on themes related to this lesson.

## Prayer

- If you completed Outreach Challenge #4, report about your experience to the group. How did it go? What did you gain from the experience?
- Ask God to provide you with opportunities to share your faith with someone this week. Report to the group any updates about the people on your prayer list, including people you've contacted and the conversations you've had.
- Pray together for your group's specific requests.

## Outreach Challenge

One of the most basic skills a Christian needs to have is the ability to explain the gospel accurately and succinctly. This week, we're challenging you to "field test" your ability to present a synopsis of the gospel to an *unchurched* friend, relative, or coworker. Take a minute right now to read through Outreach Challenge #5 (p. 89). Share your thoughts with the group about the challenge. What would prevent you from participating?

## Going Deeper

- The video sessions are based on Dr. Ross's book *Navigating Genesis*. If you'd like to explore the themes from this lesson in more detail, we suggest reading chapter 23.
- Download this week's FREE resource from RTB. In this audio message, Dr. Fazale (Fuz) Rana brings us up-to-date on key scientific discoveries that support a biblical view of humans origins. To download this resource, visit **shop.reasons.org**, click on "Audio," and then scroll down to find *The Origin of Humanity: Day 6* (MP3). Add it to your cart and use the coupon code **NavGenS6** at checkout.

---

Consider sharing one thing you learned this week or a favorite quote from the ***Navigating Genesis*** book on Facebook or Twitter.

**Use #navgen**

---

# SESSION 7

## Why Does God Rest?

# SESSION 7
# Why Does God Rest?

## Focus Verse

*By the seventh day God had finished the work he had been doing; so on the seventh day he rested from all his work.*

Genesis 2:2

## Starting the Conversation

We're continuing our search for the harmony between Scripture and nature. In this session, we'll focus our attention on **day 7**.

- Take a minute to read Genesis 2:1–3 aloud.
- Share with the group what your thoughts have been about the seventh day of creation. What do you think it means that God "rested" on the seventh day?

In this week's video presentation, Dr. Ross will discuss the harmony between nature and Scripture as it pertains to the seventh day of creation.

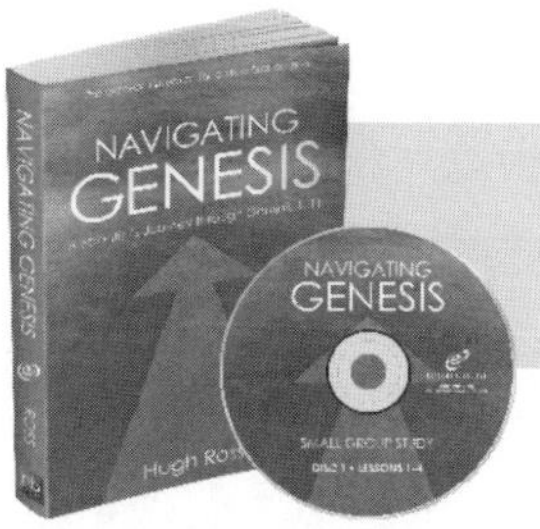


**Watch video lesson 7 now and follow along in your outline.**

## Session Outline

### › Review of the Genesis 1 creation events

Universe created (1:1)
Day 1 – Sunlight arrived on Earth's surface (1:3–5)
Day 2 – Water cycle set up (1:6–8)
Day 3 – Continents formed (1:9–10)
Day 3 – Plants appeared on continents (1:11–13)
Day 4 – Atmosphere became transparent so the Sun, Moon, and stars be came visible from Earth's surface (1:14–19)
Day 5 – Swarms of sea animals appeared (1:20–21)
Day 5 – Birds and sea mammals created (1:22–23)
Day 6 – Advanced land mammals created (1:24–25)
Day 6 – Humans created (1:26–27)

### › Accuracy of Genesis 1

- Ten creation events (see list above)
- Four initial conditions (Genesis 1:2)
    1. Dark
    2. Covered with water
    3. Empty of life
    4. Unfit for life

Evidence that Genesis (and the rest of the Bible) is the inspired, inerrant Word of God

***Notes***

## Creation Day 7

> *Thus the heavens and the earth were completed in all their vast array. By the seventh day God had finished the work he had been doing; so on the seventh day he rested from all his work.*
>
> Genesis 2:1–2

> *God saw all that he had made, and it was very good.*
>
> Genesis 1:31a

**Just as God celebrates a Sabbath rest, so should we. What should we do on the Sabbath?**

- Reflect the image of God (Genesis 1:27–28)
- Take time to enjoy and appreciate our work

**What is God doing on the seventh day?**

- God uses this creation to prepare His people for the new creation.
- God is overcoming evil (in order to ultimately eliminate it in the new creation) and bringing redemption to His people.

**How long is the seventh day?**

- No "evening" and "morning" for day seven
- Possibly still *in* the seventh day
- Long, but finite period of time

***Notes***

The seventh day is ongoing (no evening and morning mentioned).

> *"They have not known my ways." So I declared on oath in my anger, "They shall never enter my rest."*
>
> Psalm 95:10c–11

> *Jesus said to them, "My Father is always at his work to this very day, and I, too, am working."*
>
> John 5:17

> *For somewhere he has spoken about the seventh day in these words: "On the seventh day God rested from all his works."… Therefore since it still remains for some to enter that rest, and since those who formerly had the good news proclaimed to them did not go in because of their disobedience.*
>
> Hebrews 4:4, 6

**What's *not* happening on the seventh day of creation?**

- Creation of new species after the appearance of humans

**Notes**

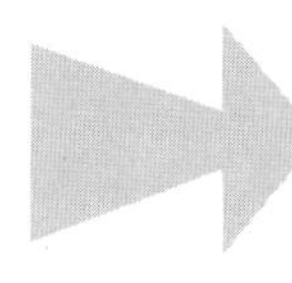

## *The Bottom Line*

The seventh day of rest means that God stopped His creation miracles, which is consistent with the fossil record. Even though God is currently resting from His creation miracles, He continues to be engaged with His world in other ways.

## Reflection

Discuss the following questions together as a group. Consider sharing relevant personal experiences so others can benefit from your situation.

- Did anyone in your group memorize the Focus Verse from session 1 (1 Peter 3:15)? Take a moment to say the verse aloud.
- In light of what you've studied in this session, what are your thoughts about God's day of rest?
- Can you think of ways that living in an urban area might inhibit our ability to see God's personal and purposeful touch in creation?
- Are you resting and taking the time to reflect upon what God allows you to create? How are you putting your creations to use for the furthering of God's kingdom?

Want to explore more science? Visit **reasons.org/navigatinggenesis** for additional articles, videos, and podcasts on themes related to this lesson.

## Prayer

- If you completed Outreach Challenge #5 this week, report your experience to the group. How did it go? What did you gain from the experience?
- Ask God to provide you with opportunities to share your faith with someone this week. Report to the group any updates about the people on your prayer list, including those you've contacted and talked with.
- Pray together for your group's specific requests.

## Outreach Challenge

Outreach Challenge #2 encouraged you to reach out to a friend and learn about their faith journey. This week's challenge builds on that encounter. We're challenging you to consider whether the time is right to take the conversation a little deeper. Take a moment right now to read through Outreach Challenge #6 (p. 91). Share your thoughts with the group. What feelings do you experience when you think about doing this challenge? What would prevent you from doing it?

## Going Deeper

- The video sessions are based on Dr. Ross's book *Navigating Genesis*. If you'd like to explore the themes from this lesson in more detail, we suggest reading chapters 7 and 9.
- Download this week's FREE resource from RTB. In this audio message, theologian and philosopher Kenneth Samples explores what the Bible means when it says that humans alone are created in the image of God. To download this resource, visit **shop.reasons.org**, click on "Audio," and then scroll down to find *The Image of God* (MP3). Add it to your cart and use the coupon code **NavGenS7** at checkout.

Consider sharing one thing you learned this week or a favorite quote from the ***Navigating Genesis*** book on Facebook or Twitter.

# SESSION 8

## Does Genesis 2 Conflict with Genesis 1?

# SESSION 8
# Does Genesis 2 Conflict with Genesis 1?

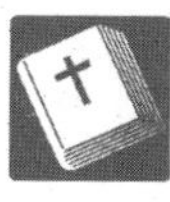

## Focus Verse

*All Scripture is God-breathed and is useful for teaching, rebuking, correcting and training in righteousness.*

2 Timothy 3:16

## Starting the Conversation

We're concluding our journey together of exploring the harmony between science and the Bible. We'll be taking a closer look at the events of **creation day 6** as they are described in **Genesis 2**.

- Take a few minutes to read Genesis 2:4–25 aloud.
- What potential contradictions do you see between Genesis 1 and 2?

Many skeptics point to the differences between the creation accounts of Genesis 1 and Genesis 2 as a challenge to the Bible's scientific accuracy. These differences seem to show inherent contradictions and, therefore, indicate that the Bible is not the error-free Word of God.

In this week's video presentation, Dr. Ross will lead us in an examination of this controversy and offer a solution.

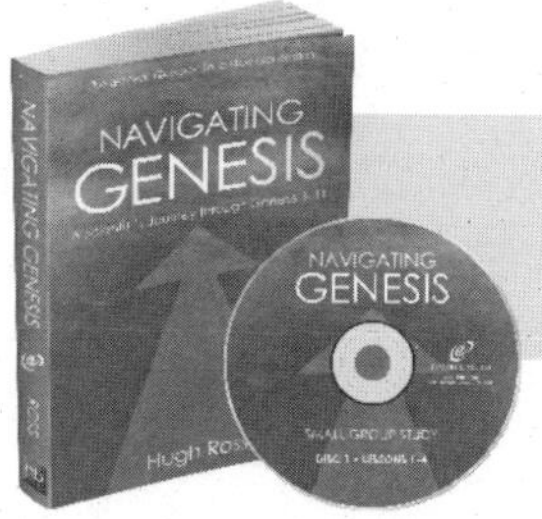


**Watch video lesson 8 now and follow along in your outline.**

## Session Outline

### › Why two accounts?

Genesis 1
- Has a physical focus
- Events arranged in chronological order

Genesis 2
- Has a spiritual focus
- Events arranged in a relational order

### › Where was the Garden of Eden?

**God introduces Adam to physical life (Genesis 2:7–8, 15–17).**
- Created outside of Eden and brought in
- Watched Eden's trees grow
- Tended the garden
- Received pleasure and some satisfaction from gardening

**God introduces Adam to the soulish creation (Genesis 2:19–20).**
- Examined all the soulish (*nepesh*) animals
- Named the animals
- Received pleasure, service, and much fulfillment from the soulish (*nepesh*) animals

**God introduces Adam to the spiritual creation (Genesis 2:18a, 20–22).**
- Of all the creatures God made, only Eve could fulfill Adam physically, soulishly, *and* spiritually.

***Notes***

- *ʿezer* (helper): defined by Carl Schultz as an "assistant in the context of a military ally or source of reinforcement for the completion of an assigned task."

### › The Great Commission

> *Therefore go and make disciples of all nations, baptizing them in the name of the Father and of the Son and of the Holy Spirit, and teaching them to obey everything I have commanded you.*
> Matthew 28:19–20a

Men and women are not the enemy. Satan is the enemy.

## *The Bottom Line*

Genesis 1 and 2 do not conflict because each serves a different purpose. Genesis 1 has a physical focus while Genesis 2 has a spiritual focus.

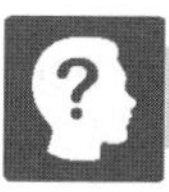

## Reflection

Discuss the following questions together as a group. Consider sharing relevant personal experiences so others can benefit from your situation.

- Did anyone in your group memorize the Focus Verse from session 1 (1 Peter 3:15)? Take a moment to say the verse aloud together.
- In light of what you've studied in this session, what are your thoughts about the creation of Eve? What difference do you think it would make if men

and women saw Satan, instead of each other, as the enemy in their efforts to bring the gospel to the ends of the earth?

- In light of what you've studied in this session, what questions do you still have about the description of the events in Genesis 2? The Going Deeper section will direct you to some additional resources.
- Describe a science-Scripture connection you made as a result of this session.

Want to explore more science? Visit **reasons.org/navigatinggenesis** for additional articles, videos, and podcasts on themes related to this lesson.

## Prayer

- If you completed Outreach Challenge #6 this week, report your experience to the group. How did it go? What did you gain from the experience?
- Report to the group any updates about the people on your prayer list, including those you've contacted and talked with.
- Pray together for your group's specific requests.

## Going Deeper

- Read through Genesis 1–3 and Revelation 20–22. Compare the similarities and differences between these two passages. In what ways will heaven be better than Eden?
- The video sessions are based on Dr. Ross's book *Navigating Genesis*. If you'd like to explore the themes from this lesson in more detail, we suggest reading chapters 8, 10, and 20.
- Download this week's FREE resource from RTB. In this audio message, you'll hear Dr. Ross use the evidences presented in this series in a real-life situation as he dialogues with atheist Michael Shermer. To download this resource, visit **shop.reasons.org**, click on "Audio," and then scroll down to

find *Responding to a Skeptic* (MP3). Add it to your cart and use the coupon code **NavGenS8** at checkout.

Consider sharing one thing you learned this week or a favorite quote from the ***Navigating Genesis*** book on Facebook or Twitter.

**Use #navgen**

# OUTREACH CHALLENGES

# Outreach Challenges

*Therefore go and make disciples of all nations, baptizing them in the name of the Father and of the Son and of the Holy Spirit, and teaching them to obey everything I have commanded you.*

Matthew 28:19–20a

In addition to being an astronomer, Hugh Ross is a seasoned pastor of evangelism. He has spent three decades serving as a missionary to scientists, skeptics, and atheists. This series of Outreach Challenges pulls from Dr. Ross's vast ministry experience and offers a roadmap to help you take steps to reach out to your nonbelieving friends and family.

This section of the study is optional. You don't need to complete these activities in order to benefit from the *Navigating Genesis* study. However, we believe that these exercises will enhance your ability to build connections with non-Christians. Even if you can't do all of the exercises, try two or three. Challenge yourself and see what new possibilities open up.

## Outreach Challenge #1

# Prayer Commitment

*Preparation* and *prayer* are critical keys to successful evangelism. Attending this eight-week series and participating in the group's discussions are the foundational steps to *preparing* yourself to interact with those who have science-faith questions.

The second step is to *pray*.

### Outreach Challenge #1

Write down the names of three non-Christian friends and family members or believers you know who are struggling with their faith. Include each person's main objection to or problem with Christianity. Then commit to pray for them for the next eight weeks.

| | Name | Faith Objection |
|---|---|---|
| 1. | ______________________ | ______________________ |
| 2. | ______________________ | ______________________ |
| 3. | ______________________ | ______________________ |

Think back to previous conversations you've had with each person. What prevents them from believing in Jesus?

- Is it the problem of evil and suffering in the world?
- Were they deeply hurt by a Christian or disgusted by hypocrisy in the church?

- Do they have a scientific or an intellectual obstacle?

Ask the Holy Spirit to begin working in their heart so that they will be open to exploring more about Christianity.

If you're comfortable with doing so, take a few minutes to share one (or more) of these names with the group so they can join you in prayer. If praying in a group is new for you or makes you uncomfortable, feel free to pray silently or just say one sentence.

"God, please help ______________ to believe in Jesus as their Savior and Creator."

## Outreach Challenge #2

# Listening Exercise

In Outreach Challenge #1, you committed to pray for three specific people during the course of this eight-week series. Outreach Challenge #2 builds on that commitment.

> **Outreach Challenge #2**
>
> Choose one person from your prayer list to contact for a meeting. If the person lives far away, consider setting up a phone call or video chat.

**During your conversation, focus on being a good *listener*.** It wouldn't be unusual if the situations that led to this person's unbelief were the result of a deeply personal situation. So, be prepared to listen to their story.

Sometimes a good place to start is **learning** about the person's religious background and his or her current spiritual status. This conversation should primarily be about **discovering** the other person's journey and his or her questions about believing in Jesus as Savior (*not* about telling your story or defending the faith).

Gently explore this person's culture, family history, and perceived arguments against Christianity. Also be prepared to listen to how this person may have been hurt by religious people.

Here are some questions to get the conversation started.

- May I ask you about your religious background/church experience?
- What were your parents' religious beliefs?
- Can you tell me about your religious beliefs now? Do you believe in a Creator or higher power?
- What do you think of Jesus? Who was He?

- How would you define Christianity?
- What do you think of Christians?
- What prevents you from being a Christian/being involved in a local church?

Focus on getting to know the person as an individual created in the image of God.

For more tips on engaging in conversations with nonbelievers, you can check out the short article below.

**Engaging with Nonbelievers**
Hugh Ross began his three-decade evangelism ministry by going door-to-door in local neighborhoods. Today, he travels the world to bring the gospel to audiences of scientists, skeptics, and atheists. Use his tips for evangelism as a roadmap to help you engage with the nonbelievers in your life.

**1. Focus on listening first.**
One of the best ways to be a good listener is by using the phrase, **"Tell me more."** Understanding the journey that led to a person's current spiritual status can provide deep insight into the underlying causes of unbelief.

Here are some additional prompts to build your listening skills.

- I'm curious to learn more about…
- Can you help me understand this part of your story better?
- Do you mind if I ask you about…?
- What I hear you saying is…
- Thanks so much for sharing your perspectives with me.

If your friend or family member is struggling, one way of showing your concern is to ask if you can pray for them.

**2. Invite skeptics to share their objections and tough questions.**
Create an environment in the relationship where the nonbeliever feels safe sharing objections without embarrassment. Part of the preparation process (1 Peter 3:15) is listening to the other person's story and questions without immediately offering a response.

Listening is not the same as *agreeing* with the other person. You can always say, "I would see it differently as a Christian, but your perspective intrigues me. Please tell me more." Over time, as trust is built, the person may begin to feel safe enough to invite you to share *your* perspective as well.

If a skeptical friend asks difficult questions about the existence of God or the reliability of the Bible, **don't feel pressured to provide all the answers**. Simply allow the person the space to ask questions and tell him or her that you'd enjoy exploring these issues together.

**3. Be authentic in your motivations.**
Non-Christians appreciate it when Christians are **honest in their intentions**. For example, if you want to invite a nonbeliever to a church outreach, be up-front about the nature and intent of the event, what will be happening, what the person might find difficult (e.g., a prayer meeting, extended worship time, etc.). Don't try to lure people to church under false pretenses. Covert witnessing is never a good idea and can lead to resentment in the relationship. Be sure to make time after the event is over to address any questions your friend may have.

Nonbelievers also appreciate it when you're up-front about your identity as a Christian. For example, simply be honest about your belief in Jesus as Creator and Savior, as opposed to appealing to an unnamed intelligent designer.

**4. There is no "slam-dunk argument" to proving there is a God.**
Many factors contribute to a person's belief system and very seldom is a person's worldview the result of an exhaustive search of evidence and testing. This means that some arguments that would be persuasive to a Western atheist might not be as compelling to a Muslim or religious Jew. Over time, you'll be well served to familiarize yourself with several worldviews.

One final note, in Dr. Ross's experience, it takes at least seven years for a research scientist to come to faith in Jesus Christ. So, if you're going to reach out to members of the scientific community, be patient. Evangelism is often more like a marathon than a sprint.

## Outreach Challenge #3

# Investigate a Question

Back in Outreach Challenge #1, we said that evangelism has two key components: *preparation* and *prayer*.

Now that we've covered prayer, let's talk about preparation.

### Outreach Challenge #3

Use the search engine at **reasons.org** to investigate one science-faith question. Listen to a podcast, read an article, or watch a video—whichever works best for you!

Ask yourself, what's one thing I can do to better **prepare myself** for future encounters with nonbelievers?

If you completed Outreach Challenge #2, then you met with one of the people on your prayer list. Perhaps that person raised a question about Christianity that you struggled to answer. Great! Here is an opportunity to explore that issue. Or perhaps you have your own questions that need answering.

Our website, **reasons.org**, is a good place to start investigating, especially if you or your friends have science-faith questions.

## Outreach Challenge #4

# Fasting

This challenge takes you to a bold next step: engaging in a period of **fasting**. Fasting is an ancient discipline practiced by Jews and Christians throughout the Bible.

> **Outreach Challenge #4**
>
> Abstain for a period of time from a luxury item or activity that you normally enjoy.

We all deprive ourselves of luxuries at certain times in order to accomplish a particular goal. Maybe we abstain from spending money so we can save to buy a car or house. We cut out high-calorie foods so we can lose weight. Perhaps we forego watching our favorite television show in order to help our kids with homework.

Fasting is a form of abstinence that allows people to become open to hearing from God in new ways. It is a biblical way of humbling oneself before God (Psalm 35:13; Ezra 8:21). The Holy Spirit will reveal your true spiritual condition, helping you recognize and repent of unconfessed sins. Fasting will also open up more time in your day to pray for unsaved friends.

Historically, fasting has been connected to abstaining from food, but total abstinence is not always necessary. For example, you could decide to fast from "luxury foods" such as meat or sugar, much like Daniel and the young men of Israel did in Babylon (Daniel 1).

It is also possible to fast from nonfood items. You could engage in a media or Internet fast. Although many of us need to use computers as part of our jobs and we need phones to communicate, we also engage in additional media just to pass the time. Consider cutting out any media that isn't vital for your job or communication.

Be sure to focus on what you will use to *replace* the luxury item. Here are some ideas for when you find yourself missing that luxury item.

- Pray for the people on your prayer list.
- Read a book of the Bible or a book on apologetics.
- Memorize this week's Focus Verse.
- Meditate on 1 Peter 3:15.

Ask God to bring to mind a particular time when you *didn't* act with gentleness and respect toward an nonbeliever. Then ask God for forgiveness. Also, consider how you can make amends with that person by going to them and asking for their forgiveness (Matthew 5:23–24).

The length of your fasting time is up to you. We recommend a week, but yours could be longer or shorter. Also consider inviting your family to join in the experience.

Don't forget to share with your group what you learned from this experience. What did you notice as you abstained from a luxury item?

## Outreach Challenge #5

# Field Test

One of the most basic evangelism skills a Christian needs is the ability to explain the gospel accurately and succinctly. This week, we're challenging you to "field test" your ability to present a synopsis of the gospel to one of the people on your prayer list. If you can't connect with any of them, reach out to a non-Christian friend, relative, or coworker.

### Outreach Challenge #5

Present the facts of the gospel in a straightforward manner that is understandable to an unchurched person.

This is *not* an effort to evangelize. Your goal is to present the gospel in two minutes or less in order to receive feedback about how you did so you can improve. You might find it helpful to first write out your gospel presentation (2–3 paragraphs).

It should answer the following questions:

- What is salvation?
- Why do people need salvation?
- What do people need to be saved from?
- How can people be saved?

Assume that the person listening to you has absolutely no knowledge of the biblical teaching on salvation or the Bible. Thus, if you use any Christian terms, remember to explain them briefly and clearly. Creativity is a plus here. If you *really* want to challenge yourself, avoid using the following expressions or explanations in your presentation.

- Your personal testimony or experience
- "Accept Jesus in my heart to be my Savior and Lord"
- "Blind faith" or "just believe" (faith not based on evidence)
- Humanity's main need is for "meaning" and "purpose" in life
- Salvation fills a "God-shaped hole" in our heart

Be sure to explain to your listener up front that you are merely looking for feedback. Emphasize that this **isn't a covert attempt to convert them** to Christianity.

After your presentation, don't forget to ask your friend for feedback.

- Was the presentation understandable?
- If not, which parts needed more clarity?

When receiving feedback, resist the urge to argue or respond defensively. Just listen.

In the days that follow, ponder the listener's feedback. Do you think the comments had any merit? Do you see any truth there? Share with your group what you learned from this experience. What kind of feedback did you receive? What did you struggle with the most?

## Outreach Challenge #6

# Resource Discussion

Outreach Challenge #2 encouraged you to reach out to a friend or family member to learn about that person's faith journey. This week's challenge builds on that encounter.

The first step in this challenge is to consider whether it's a good time to take the conversation with this person to a deeper level. If the time is right, we suggest that you and your friend each select a resource to discuss together. Then discuss the ideas presented in both resources. Remember to do this in a way that promotes gentleness and respect.

Offer to read a book, watch a DVD, or listen to a podcast of your friend's choice first. Be prepared for your friend to choose something that's not familiar to you. Your resource will likely be unfamiliar to your friend as well.

When it's your turn to offer a resource, if possible, suggest one that addresses your friend's main objection to Christianity. You can access a variety of free resources (podcasts, articles, and videos) for science-faith issues at **reasons.org**—just use the search engine at the top of the screen or click "Explore" to search by topic, resource type, or author. For books, DVDs, and other more in-depth resources, click "Shop" to browse the RTB web store.

If the relationship isn't ready for this step, don't sweat it. Instead, take time to dig deeper into the topics covered in this study and prepare yourself for future conversations with non-Christians.

# Where Do We Go From Here?

Congratulations! You've finished the *Navigating Genesis* small group study. We hope this series has enriched your spiritual life and helped you grow in your confidence to share the gospel with others.

As you close, please consider taking additional steps to help you learn more about Jesus as the Creator and Savior.

- Consider holding a ninth session in which you and your fellow participants focus on sharing what God has done in your life through this study. This could also be a time to invite new friends to hear your testimonials and encourage them to do the study with you next time.
- If you skipped the Outreach Challenges, set a goal to complete them in the next three weeks.
- Finish reading Hugh Ross's book *Navigating Genesis*. It covers Genesis chapters 3–11.
- Consider leading the *Navigating Genesis* study with a different group.
- Explore RTB's other small group studies, including *If God Made the Universe* (also with Dr. Ross) or *The Bigger Picture on Creation*, which offers a more in-depth inductive Bible study of Genesis 1–2.
- Explore RTB's extensive library of articles, videos, and podcasts at **reasons.org**.
- Take an online course through Reasons Institute. For more information, visit **reasonsinstitute.com**.

**Has this study impacted your life?**
Hugh Ross and the rest of the RTB team would love to hear how this series and the book *Navigating Genesis* have helped you. Please share your story with us by emailing **navigatinggenesis@reasons.org**.